How to Write a Thank-You Letter

by Cecilia Minden
and Kate Roth

THANK YOU!

CHERRY LAKE PUBLISHING · ANN ARBOR, MICHIGAN

CHERRY LAKE
Publishing

Published in the United States of America by Cherry Lake Publishing
Ann Arbor, Michigan
www.cherrylakepublishing.com

Content Adviser: Gail Dickinson, PhD, Associate Professor, Old Dominion University,
Norfolk, Virginia

Photo Credits: Page 7, ©wavebreakmedia ltd/Shutterstock, Inc.; page 9, ©Darrin
Henry/Shutterstock, Inc.; page 17, ©iStockphoto.com/ktaylorg; page 20, ©AVAVA/
Shutterstock, Inc.

Library of Congress Cataloging-in-Publication Data
Minden, Cecilia.
  How to write a thank you letter / by Cecilia Minden and Kate Roth.
    p. cm. — (Language arts explorer junior)
  Includes bibliographical references and index.
  ISBN 978-1-61080-489-9 (lib. bdg.) —
ISBN 978-1-61080-576-6 (e-book) — ISBN 978-1-61080-663-3 (pbk.)
1. Thank-you notes—Juvenile literature. 2. Letter writing—Juvenile literature.
3. English language—Composition and exercises—Juvenile literature.
I. Roth, Kate. II. Title.
  BJ2115.T45M56 2012
  395.4–dc23   2012005748

Cherry Lake Publishing would like to acknowledge the work
of The Partnership for 21st Century Skills. Please visit
www.21stcenturyskills.org for more information.

Printed in the United States of America
Corporate Graphics Inc.
July 2012
CLFA11

THANK YOU!

Table of Contents

CHAPTER ONE

Why Write a Thank-You Note?

A thank-you note tells others that we are grateful for what they did for us. It is a way of giving back for what we've received. Think about the last time someone thanked you. Didn't you feel good to hear or read such kind words? A thank-you note is a great way to let others know that you appreciate them.

This book will help you learn to write two kinds of thank-you notes:

- Thank you for a gift
- Thank you for an **event**

Writing thank-you notes shows good manners.

All thank-you notes have five main parts:

1. Date (the day, month, and year the note was written)
2. **Greeting** (words that begin the letter)
3. **Body** (the main part of the letter)
4. **Closing** (words that end the letter)
5. **Signature** (the letter writer's name, written by hand)

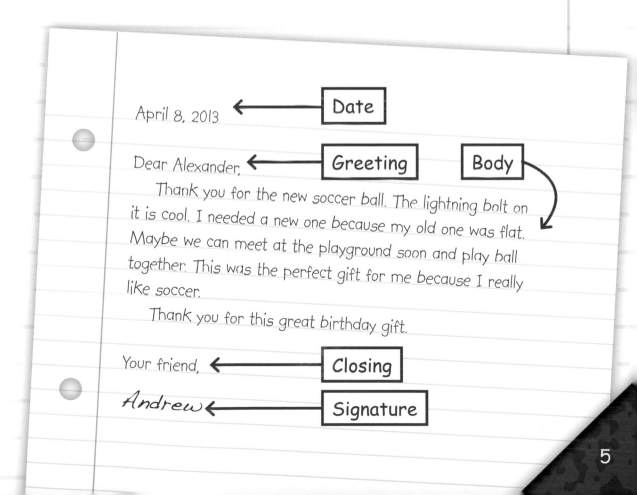

You can have a lot of fun designing and writing thank-you notes. They can be written on small, colorful notepaper or cards. The envelope can match the notepaper. Some people like to decorate the card with stickers or drawings.

Here is what you will need to complete the activities in this book:

- Clean notebook paper for your **draft**
- Notepaper or cards
- **Envelopes**
- Stamps
- A pencil with an eraser
- A pen

Even if a card says "Thank You!" on the front, you should still write a note inside.

CHAPTER TWO

Thank You for the Gift!

Think carefully about the gift you are writing about.

Think about your gift when you begin to write the thank-you note. How will you use your gift? Is it something to read, play with, or wear? Is it something you can share with others? Make a list of at least three different things you can say about your gift. This information will help you tell the gift giver exactly why you are so thankful for the gift. You want the gift giver to know you are writing just to him or her.

ACTIVITY

Make a List

In this activity you will make a list of what you like about the gift.

INSTRUCTIONS:
1. Write the name of the gift.
2. Write down at least three things you like about the gift.

Send your thank-you note within a few days of getting the gift.

Gift: a book from Aunt CC
- The story was about a trip to a fire station.
- My dad is a firefighter.
- I like to visit my Dad's fire station.
- I like to read with my mom and dad.

To get a copy of this activity, visit www.cherrylakepublishing.com/activities.

CHAPTER THREE

Dear Aunt CC

Be sure to follow all of the steps for writing a proper letter.

Now you have a clear idea about why you liked your gift. Use your list to write a draft of your thank-you note.

Begin a thank-you note by writing the date at the top of the page. Leave a blank line under the date, then write the greeting. The greeting begins with "Dear" and then the person's name. Put a comma after the name. Drop down to the next line and **indent** to begin your first **paragraph**. Your first sentence should include the words "Thank you for" and name the gift. Now turn your list into several sentences. Let the person know how much you enjoy the gift and why you like it. End the note by writing the closing, such as "Sincerely" or "Your friend." Then sign your name.

Examples of closings are Love, Thank you again, and Yours truly. The first letter of the first word is a capital letter.

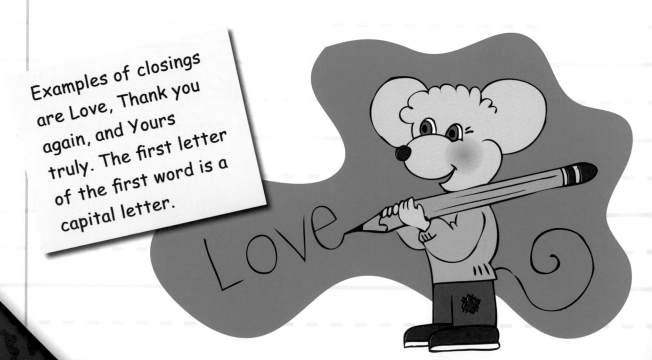

To get a copy of this activity, visit www.cherrylakepublishing.com/activities.

ACTIVITY

Write the Thank-You Note

In this activity you will write a thank-you note for a gift.

INSTRUCTIONS:
1. Start by writing a draft. Write the date at the top of a piece of paper.
2. On the next line, write the greeting "Dear" and the name of the person who gave you the gift.
3. Put a comma after the person's name.
4. Begin the body of the letter by writing "Thank you for" and the name of the gift.
5. Use your list about why you liked the gift to write several sentences.
6. Write a closing.
7. Put a comma after the closing words.
8. Look over your draft to make sure there are no mistakes. Make sure there is nothing you want to add.
9. Copy your draft in your best handwriting to the notepaper.
10. Sign your name.

Activity continued on page 12

Activity continued from page 11.

September 17, 2013

Dear Aunt CC,
    Thank you for the books. I read them with my mom and dad. They liked them, too. My favorite book was *The Fire Truck Adventure*. My favorite part was when Herbie dreamt about being a firefighter. My dad is a firefighter. He lets me pretend to drive the fire truck and turn on the lights. It is really fun.

Thank you again,
William

CHAPTER FOUR

Thank You for Inviting Me!

You should also write thank-you notes after someone invites you to a party or other event. Before you write, make a list of everything you did together. Maybe your grandma took you out for ice cream on a hot day. Make a list of why you liked this activity and what made it special. Your grandma will enjoy remembering what you did together. Your note will also let her know that you are grateful for a fun time.

Ice cream is a great treat on a hot day!

To get a copy of this activity, visit www.cherrylakepublishing.com/activities.

ACTIVITY

Make a List

In this activity you will make a list of things you liked about the event.

INSTRUCTIONS:
1. Write the name of the event.
2. Write down at least three things you liked about the event.

Send your thank-you note within a few days of the event.

Event: Ice-cream date with Grandma
- My favorite ice-cream place
- Shared a sundae
- We both like sprinkles and whipped cream
- Great way to spend a hot day

CHAPTER FIVE

Dear Grandma

This thank-you note looks like the one you wrote for your gift. It has the same five main parts of a letter. Put the date and greeting at the top. Indent and write your paragraph. Use your list to help you remember all the things you want to say. Let the person know you were happy to be invited to such a fun event. Be sure you include something that happened while you were together. This makes your thank-you note special. End the note with a closing and sign your name.

ACTIVITY

Write the Thank-You Note

In this activity you will write a thank-you note to someone who showed you a good time.

Activity continued on page 16

Activity continued from page 15.

INSTRUCTIONS:

1. Start by writing a draft. Write the date at the top of a piece of paper.
2. On the next line, write the greeting "Dear" and the name of the person who hosted the event.
3. Put a comma after the person's name.
4. Begin the body of the letter by writing "Thank you for" and the name of event.
5. Use your list about why you liked the activity to write several sentences.
6. Write a closing.
7. Put a comma after the closing words.
8. Look over your draft to make sure there are no mistakes. Make sure there is nothing you want to add.
9. Copy your draft in your best handwriting to the notepaper.
10. Sign your name.

Did you take photos at the event? Include one in your thank-you note.

July 12, 2013

Dear Grandma,

Thank you for taking me to get ice cream at my favorite place. I loved sharing the chocolate sundae with you. I am glad you like whipped cream and sprinkles just like me. It was a great way to spend a hot summer day. I hope to see you again soon.

Hugs from me,
Annabel

CHAPTER SIX

Signed, Sealed, and Stamped

Once you've addressed and stamped the envelope, you're ready to send your letter.

Now you are ready to mail your thank-you note. Write your name and address in the upper left-hand corner on the envelope. Write the full name of the person receiving the thank-you note in the middle of the envelope. Write his or her address under the name. Write clearly so the

post office will know where to send the letter.
Stick a stamp in the upper right-hand corner.

Address and Stamp the Envelope

In this activity you will address the envelope.

INSTRUCTIONS:
1. The **seal flap** of the envelope should be at the top.
2. Be sure to write on the front of the envelope.
3. Write your name and address in the upper left corner.
4. Write the name and address of the person receiving the note in the center of the envelope.
5. Put a stamp in the upper right corner.

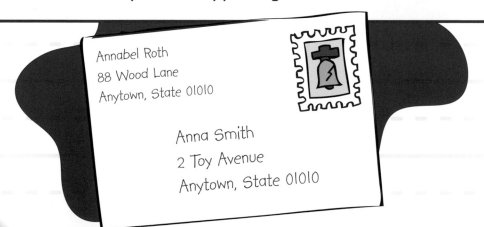

STOP!
DON'T WRITE
IN THE BOOK!

ACTIVITY

Final Changes

☐ YES ☐ NO Do I start my letter with today's date?

☐ YES ☐ NO Do I include a greeting?

☐ YES ☐ NO Do I explain why I like the gift or enjoyed the event?

☐ YES ☐ NO Do I include a closing and signature?

☐ YES ☐ NO Do I include photos if I have any?

☐ YES ☐ NO Do I address the envelope correctly?

☐ YES ☐ NO Do I remember to put a stamp on the envelope?

To get a copy of the activities on this spread, visit www.cherrylakepublishing.com/activities.

CHAPTER SEVEN

Other Ways to Say Thank You

Your friends and relatives will be thrilled to get your thank-you notes through e-mail.

It is nice to send a thank-you note in the mail. However, there are other ways to send a thank you:

- Send an e-mail.
- Stick a thank-you note in someone's pocket or locker as a surprise.
- Put a thank-you note in someone's book, lunch bag, or desk.

People do good deeds every day. It is nice to thank them for what they do. Who knows? You may receive a thank you for your thank you!

Everyone loves to get thank-you notes!

Glossary

body (BAH-dee) the main part of a letter

closing (KLOH-zing) the words that end a letter

draft (DRAFT) a first version of a document, or one that is not final

envelopes (ON-vuh-lohpss) flat paper coverings that are used to mail letters

event (eh-VENT) something of importance that happens

greeting (GREE-ting) the opening words of a letter, such as "Dear Sally"

indent (in-DEHNT) to start a line of writing farther in from the left edge of a page than the other lines

paragraph (PARE-uh-graf) a group of sentences about a certain idea or subject

seal flap (SEEL FLAP) the part of an envelope that folds down to close it

signature (SIG-nuh-chur) a person's name signed by hand

For More Information

BOOK

Summers, Jean. *The Kids' Guide to Writing Great Thank-You Notes.*
Cranston, RI: Writers Collective, 2006.

WEB SITE
KidsPrintables.com
www.kidprintables.com/thankyounotes
Use these fun designs to create your thank-you notes.

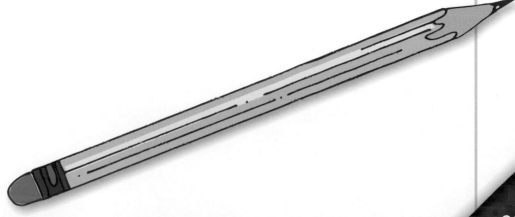

Index

About the Authors

Cecilia Minden, PhD, is the former director of the Language and Literacy Program at Harvard Graduate School of Education. She earned her doctorate from the University of Virginia. While at Harvard, Dr. Minden also taught several writing courses. Her research focused on early literacy skills and developing phonics curricula. She is now an educational consultant and the author of more than 100 books for children. Dr. Minden lives with her family in Chapel Hill, North Carolina. She likes to write early in the morning while the house is still quiet.

Kate Roth has a doctorate from Harvard University in language and literacy and a master's from Columbia University Teachers College in curriculum and teaching. Her work focuses on writing instruction in the primary grades. She has taught first grade, kindergarten, and Reading Recovery. She has also instructed hundreds of teachers from around the world in early literacy practices. She lives in Shanghai, China, with her husband and three children, ages 3, 7, and 10. Her two oldest children, Annabel and Andrew, wrote the thank-you letters used in this book.